STARK LIBRARY APR

MW01201364

DISCARD

Patience...

Rachel Williams　　　　Leonie Lord

MAGIC CAT 🐱 PUBLISHING

NEW YORK

WHY WAIT?

The word *PATIENCE* comes from the Latin word patientia, meaning
"to endure" or "to wait." It can happen when we practice slowing down to think
about the natural process of life. Some things might happen in a day, a year,
or even 100 years, and it can sometimes feel like one long waiting game . . .

ARE WE THERE YET?

WHEN WILL THE BABY BE BORN?

HOW MANY DAYS UNTIL CHRISTMAS?

WHEN WILL I GROW TALLER?

HOW LONG UNTIL GRANDPA'S BIRTHDAY?

IS IT DINNER TIME?!

But in life, *PATIENCE* is essential while we wait for important things to take place.

We live in a world where fantastic technology exists, so it's natural to want all the answers *right now*—and for everything to happen immediately. But it's important to enjoy the journey and leave plenty of space for discovery.

This book has been written as an antidote to our instant world. It's also a reminder that some of the most magical things in life—from the beat of your heart, to the growth of a whole rainforest—take time and are full of *WONDER*.

CONTENTS

IN ONE MINUTE

Your heart beats 60-100 times

Place your hand in the middle of your chest.
Do you feel it? *Lup-dub, lup-dub, lup-dub . . .* it's your
heartbeat! Your heart is hard at work, pumping blood
around your body, making sure it gets all the oxygen
and nutrients it needs to survive.

In just one minute, blood circulates throughout your
entire body. In just one day, your heart may beat
around 100,000 times! And it beats even faster if
you're young and running around. But whether you're
playing or resting, awake, or asleep, your heart is busy
beating away. *Lup-dub, lup-dub, lup-dub . . .*

At every living moment, your heart beats and beats . . .

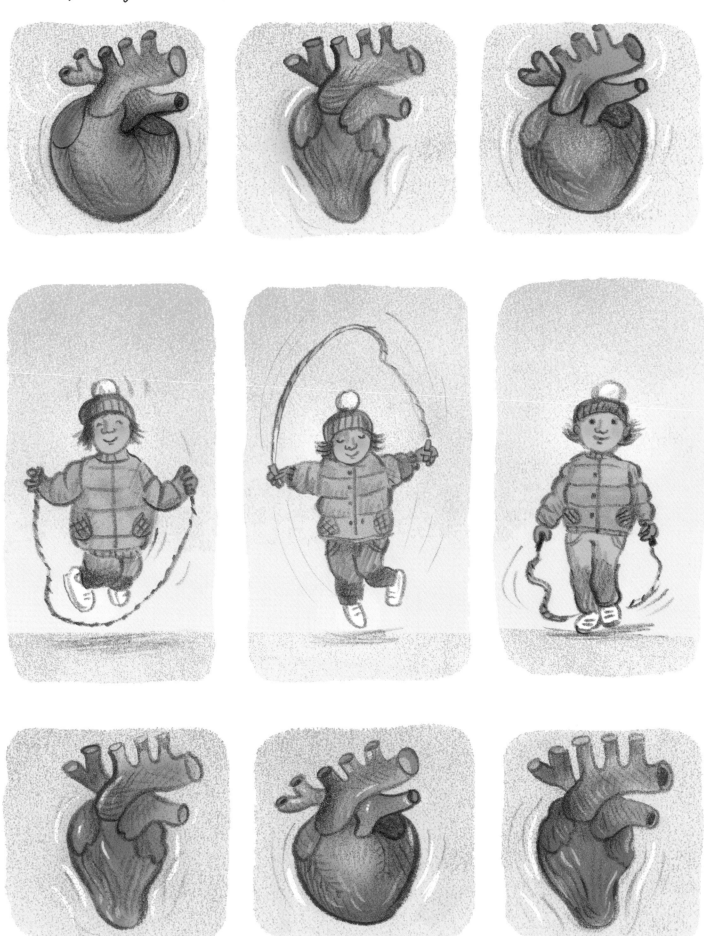

. . . pumping blood throughout your body.

ONE MINUTE, BEAT TO BEAT

When you're on the move your heart beats even quicker, moving blood to all the muscles that need oxygen and nutrients to work.

Every time you skip over a jump rope, your heart squeezes tight and then relaxes, sending blood rushing through your body to your jumping legs, strong arms, and busy brain. This process is called *CIRCULATION*.

With every breath you take, your lungs fill with oxygen . . . and your heart keeps *BEATING!*

Blood carrying oxygen from your lungs enters the left side of your heart through the pulmonary vein. Your heart beats, and the blood rushes through your **AORTIC VALVE** and out into the **BLOOD VESSELS**.

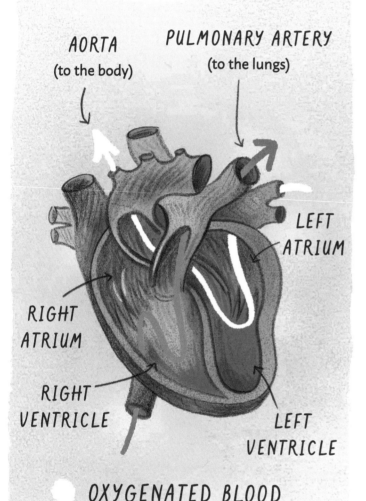

AORTA
(to the body)

PULMONARY ARTERY
(to the lungs)

LEFT ATRIUM

RIGHT ATRIUM

RIGHT VENTRICLE

LEFT VENTRICLE

○ OXYGENATED BLOOD

● DEOXYGENATED BLOOD

Once your body has used up all the oxygen, the blood rushes all the way back, into the right side of your heart. It needs fresh oxygen, so it passes through your **PULMONARY ARTERY** and into your lungs, ready to start the whole cycle again.

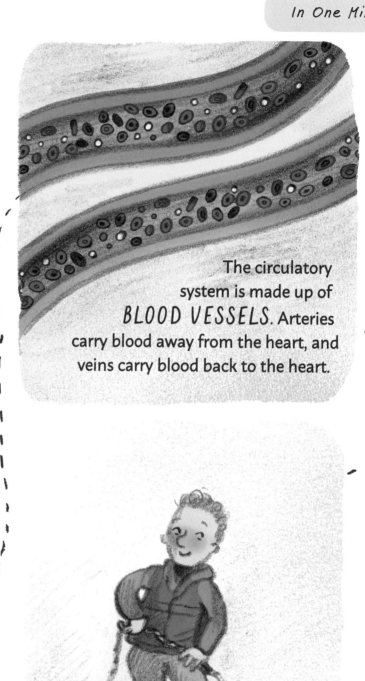

The circulatory system is made up of **BLOOD VESSELS**. Arteries carry blood away from the heart, and veins carry blood back to the heart.

And in one fun-filled minute of skipping, your heart has beaten over 100 times. Phew!

There are four chambers in your heart: the left and right **VENTRICLES** at the bottom, and the left and right **ATRIUMS** at the top.

9

IN EIGHT MINUTES

- -

Light from the sun reaches Earth

A lot can happen in eight minutes. You can prepare a bowl of oatmeal or boil a pot of spaghetti. In that same time, light from the sun reaches Earth, traveling a truly mind-blowing distance of about 93 million miles through space before we get to see it.

At the center of our solar system is the sun, the closest star to our planet. This giant ball of glowing gases provides light, warmth, and energy to all life on Earth, helping us stay healthy and happy. Without the sun, we would not exist!

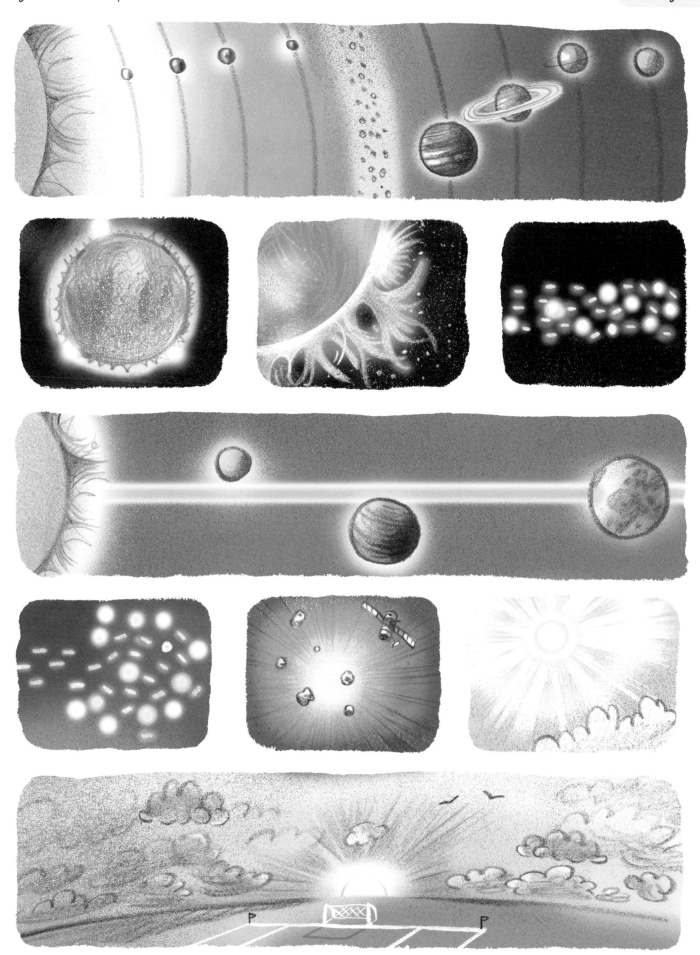

. . . reaching Earth as a sunbeam!

EIGHT MINUTES *to* LIGHT

Millions of miles away from the sun, a soccer game is underway.

While the players are running around on the field, a special energetic reaction is happening at the sun's core—*PHOTONS* are being created.

These little packets of energy escape to the sun's surface, bouncing off *ELECTRONS*, a bit like a soccer ball being passed around on the grass.

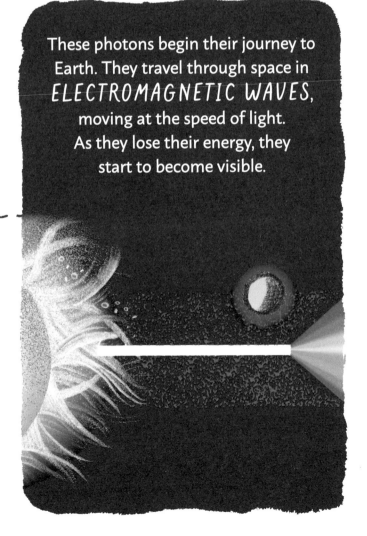

These photons begin their journey to Earth. They travel through space in *ELECTROMAGNETIC WAVES*, moving at the speed of light. As they lose their energy, they start to become visible.

Like players dodging their opponents and making a beeline for the goal, photons avoid planets, satellites, and space debris as they enter EARTH'S ATMOSPHERE in a straight line.

LIGHT moves faster than anything else in the universe—some 186,000 miles per second!

Eight minutes later, the photons hit the soccer field—and the crowd watching—sending signals to every living thing on Earth that there is light. And before long, a GOAL is scored!

IN ONE HOUR

A barn owl hunts its prey

The wind rustles in the woods on this warm evening. Suddenly, a brown-and-white barn owl swoops from the branches of the biggest oak tree to a fence post, landing without a sound. Always on the watch, he has waited for dusk to fall before he begins his hunt . . .

Every evening for at least an hour, Barn Owl stalks the wild open countryside where he has the best chance of catching prey. To succeed, he relies on his light-sensitive vision and sharp sense of hearing. His heart-shaped face captures the slightest sound, collecting and directing it toward his inner ears, which sit just behind his wide eyes.

As dusk falls, the hunt begins.

ONE-HOUR HUNT

As the light begins to fade, a hungry field vole scurries through the long, rough grassland.

We can barely see him as he darts in and out of cover. But far above him, a *BARN OWL* is scouring the land for his next meal.

The evening is still—perfect conditions for Barn Owl to pick up even the quietest squeak or rustle. He flies back and forth for up to an hour, *SURVEYING* the ground below for small mammals such as mice, rats, shrews, and voles.

It's getting darker, but this doesn't hinder Barn Owl, who is now HOVERING above one patch, as though frozen mid-flight. He has spotted a FIELD VOLE. He tracks the vole with intent. He needs to be patient . . .

Suddenly, Barn Owl pulls back his great wings and SWOOPS down to the ground in near silence, his talons thrust forward. He takes the vole by surprise—the tiny mammal stands no chance against such speed and accuracy.

With his catch secured, Barn Owl heads back to his nest to enjoy his supper, as dusk turns to night.

BARN OWLS use a hunting method called QUARTERING. They fly back and forth in sections, scanning the land below for up to an hour to locate and catch their prey.

IN ONE NIGHT

The moon rises and falls

Night falls, and the moon rises high above the horizon. As the hours pass sleepily by, the glowing sphere moves steadily across the sky, before dropping back down again just before the dawn . . .

Every night, Earth's only natural satellite travels in a continuous arc, shining brightly as it reflects light from the sun. And even though the moon seems to disappear for a couple of nights each month, it is still there, going to "sleep" and "rising to shine," just like you.

ONE NIGHT IN THE LIFE *of* THE MOON

In the evening, as dusk falls, the full moon sets off on a magical journey . . .

As bedtime arrives, a bright white light fills the window, illuminating the night sky. Tonight, the once-a-month moon appears . . . a *FULL MOON*!

The *MOON* climbs a little higher above Earth. As it gets higher still it turns to pale orange, brightening the black sky as your eyelids slowly fall . . .

When the comfort of rest sets in, the moon arches across the sky. It may look like it's shining on Earth below, but it is actually *REFLECTING* different amounts of sunlight as it moves around (orbits) Earth.

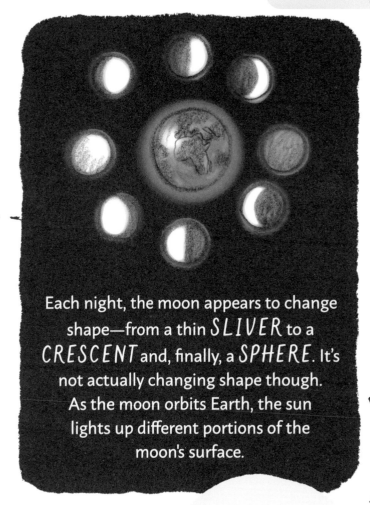

Each night, the moon appears to change shape—from a thin *SLIVER* to a *CRESCENT* and, finally, a *SPHERE*. It's not actually changing shape though. As the moon orbits Earth, the sun lights up different portions of the moon's surface.

MOONRISE and MOONSET are the moments when the upper edge of the moon peeks above the horizon and then passes below it. This happens every night of the year!

Finally, the moon falls toward the *HORIZON*. Here, it sets, disappearing out of sight. And before long, another new day will dawn.

IN ONE DAY

- - - - - - - - - - - - - - - -

A dragonfly gets ready to fly

After a long, hot day on the riverbank, there is still much activity in the early evening light. A tiny insect darts back and forth along the water's edge, moving at lightning speed. As it hovers above a reed, you notice its sleek black body and dashes of yellow—it's a black darter dragonfly!

Like all species of dragonfly, the black darter nymph hatches from an egg laid in or near to water. The nymph remains submerged, gorging on tadpoles, small fish, and other insects. Once it is almost fully grown, it prepares to surface, ready to take to the skies.

Tiny wings grow . . .

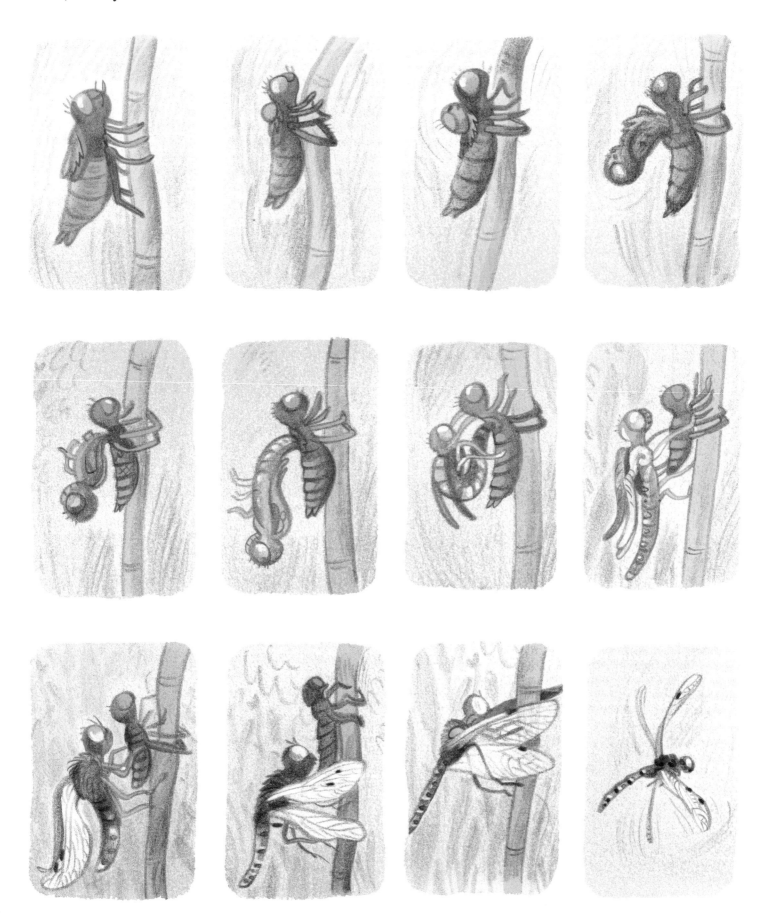

. . . into big wings!

A DAY BY THE RIVERBANK

A well-trodden path through the long grass leads to a quiet spot on the *RIVERBANK*. The river glistens as little fish swish around above the pebbles in the clear water.

A gentle breeze makes a shushing sound as it touches the reeds and rushes. On one reed, a tiny *NYMPH* is resting, having spent the night slinking up and out of the water to find the perfect spot to begin its *TRANSFORMATION*.

The nymph starts to shed its outer shell. Its *EXOSKELETON* cracks open and the bright body inside births, curling backward until it is upside down, hanging on by the very tip of its abdomen. You're so busy paddling, you don't even see the newly emerged black darter dragonfly in these final stages of *METAMORPHOSIS*.

Dragonflies are **SPEEDY ACROBATS**. They can dart in all directions and hover in the same spot, reaching speeds of up to 35 miles an hour.

The **DRAGONFLY** waits patiently until its body dries and it's stable enough to fully open up. Soon, it unfolds four perfect wings!

After a full day, the dragonfly is almost ready to take flight. As the evening sets in, it hovers for a moment in the air before whizzing off on its first adventure...

IN TWELVE DAYS

A blackbird incubates her eggs

The cool spring air is alive with birdsong. Over several days, a noisy bird has been busy building a nest in a local tree. As she flits back and forth, filling the nest with grass, pine needles, and soft leaves, her glossy black feathers catch the light, making them shimmer green and purple.

She has carefully constructed a safe, cozy nest for her babies, who are still safely enclosed in their eggs. For the next twelve days she will bear the duty of sitting on her eggs, keeping them at the perfect temperature, until the first of the chicks is ready to hatch. Then, her partner will help feed their hungry brood . . .

Building a nest . . .

. . . to build a family!

NESTING THE DAYS AWAY . . .

Outside in the garden, a blackbird finishes constructing the strong outer layer of a nest. She adds a soft, downy feather lining. She flits back and forth, making sure the nesting place is just right.

When she returns to her nest for the evening, Mother Blackbird will settle in to lay five perfect pale blue eggs. Under the warmth of her belly, the *EMBRYOS* inside these shells will start to develop.

Mother Blackbird lifts herself up and shuffles the eggs around, making sure that each one gets her attention, before she settles back down again for the night.

In the morning, Father Blackbird returns to the nest, bringing food for his mate—a few small seeds and a juicy worm to eat.

For the next twelve days, this routine continues. Soon, tiny fractures appear on the smooth surface of the eggs . . .

Peck, peck, peck . . . The cracks widen, and soon little beaks can be seen!

Shells burst apart, and featherless CHICKS emerge. Now, both parents must keep their new chicks well fed and safe until they are strong enough to leave the nest . . .

Songbirds, like BLACKBIRDS, are also known as PERCHING BIRDS. Within the bird world, these birds have the shortest incubation time (usually 10–15 days). Hens incubate their eggs for 21 days, ducks for 28 days. Meanwhile, a giant albatross egg takes up to 80 days to hatch!

IN TWO WEEKS

- - - - - - - - - - - - - - - - -

A camel crosses the desert to drink

As the sun sets on another sweltering day in the desert, a silhouette appears on the horizon: a dromedary camel! The dark shapes, each with a single hump, tall legs, and elongated neck, grow in number as they move slowly and rhythmically across the dusty landscape in a long train.

The water stored in the camel's bloodstream is depleting, and soon they will need to find water to replenish their stores. In a single thirsty stop-off, they will each guzzle over 30 gallons in just 15 minutes before continuing on their journey, fully nourished. Even when all around is barren, these camels know they have everything they need to survive until the next, faraway stop . . .

Day One, and the search for water begins . . .

. . . until water is found.

A TWO-WEEK JOURNEY

The sun blazes down on the desert at the break of day.
Here, a caravan of camels rest and drink before they
embark on the long walk that stretches out before them.

As they do before all their journeys, the camels arch
their long necks down toward a welcome watering hole.
Submerging their mouths, they suck up massive gulps of water.

As the group, or caravan, of camels drink on, their
long eyelashes shield their eyes from the sand
being whipped up by the breeze.

The camels' thick coats help to regulate their body temperature in these extreme conditions.

DROMEDARY CAMELS don't store water in their humps but rather fat, which they convert into energy and water when needed, providing nourishment on long, hot journeys when sustenance is nowhere to be found.

Slowly, steadily, the *HUMPS*, like the sand dunes, move up and down as the camels pad away, before fading into the hazy horizon.

They will pace themselves over the next two weeks until they reach their next watering hole.

IN ONE MONTH

The moon completes a lunar cycle

High up in the sky, more than 200,000 miles above us, the moon is the shiny orb that never rests. Over the course of almost a month, the moon will orbit Earth. And as it travels, it appears to change shape, from a silver sliver to a bright oval, and finally a bountiful ball. Then, like a magic trick, it will disappear . . . only to return and repeat the cycle all over again next month.

Tonight, the majestic moon is ready to begin its journey once more, through eight spectacular shape-shifting phases . . .

A MONTH OF MOON WATCHING

Tonight, the night sky is dark, except for the blanket of stars high above: here is the *NEW MOON*. But then, a small, shiny sliver appears from behind a cloud: a *WAXING CRESCENT*! It looks like it's glowing, but it's actually sunlight reflecting off the moon's face.

A week has passed by, and now we start to make out the details of the *FIRST QUARTER MOON*. Half of the moon's face is now illuminated. You can even make out the gray and white patches of the steep mountains and low, rocky plains that make up the moon's surface.

Day 10, and an oval shape now glows. *WAXING GIBBOUS MOON* is bursting to fill the night sky!

It takes the moon 27.3 days to orbit Earth, but because Earth is moving at the same time, it takes approximately 29.5 days for the moon to go through its eight different phases—a *LUNAR MONTH*.

At Day 14, the **FULL MOON** arrives in all its glory, taking center stage among the specks of stars and satellites. How fortunate to see such an impressive sight every month!

After the excitement of the last couple of days, **WANING GIBBOUS MOON** starts to shrink, getting smaller by the day.

By Day 22, the moon reaches its **THIRD QUARTER PHASE**, appearing like half a glazed pie in the sky. As the days go by, the darkness edges farther and farther across the moon's face . . .

It is Day 26 now, and the night engulfs the **WANING CRESCENT MOON**, with one small slip of light remaining. After about 29.5 days, the moon fades entirely to black, becoming a new moon once more.

OVER MANY MONTHS

A honeypot ant stores food

Deep within the twisting tunnels of an underground nest,
a colony of honeypot ants have been hard at work. While
other insects, like honey bees and wasps, store food in their
nests, these ants are truly unique: They use their own bodies
as living food storage.

Throughout autumn, the colony's foragers work tirelessly above
ground, searching for precious plant sap and liquid nectar.
When they've gathered all they can, they return to the nest to
feed the repletes—the worker ants whose abdomens swell to
hold the sugary sap for later use. Come wintertime, when food
is scarce, the replete ants regurgitate the nectars so that the
colony has everything it needs to survive . . .

A forager ant searches for sap over many months . . .

. . . returning each day to feed its family.

39

MONTHS *of* THIRSTY WORK

The sun has long been up, and a small team of honeypot worker ants are on the hunt for breakfast. Scurrying across the scorched terrain, they march in line toward a cactus.

They take all the sweet *NECTAR* they can from the cactus flowers and make their way back to the nest.

In the deepest part of the *NEST*, they enter a cavernous area filled with what look like golden droplets. But these are their siblings!

The worker ants regurgitate the gathered nectar a drop at a time, transferring it to the *REPLETES*, who are hanging upside down.

But the worker ants' task is not yet over, and they venture out again. They will **REPEAT** this process until the repletes back at the nest are filled right up— swollen, and a golden honey color.

After many months of **HARVESTING**, the weather cools and food becomes more scarce. But the honeypot ants know there are enough resources back at the nest to survive the winter.

Finally, all their hard work pays off. The repletes **REGURGITATE** their sweet stores so that all the nest-mates can enjoy the sugary harvest.

The **REPLETE** stays still until a hungry ant begs for food by stroking her **ANTENNAE**. She responds by opening her mouth and regurgitating the food. This is known as **TROPHALLAXIS**.

41

IN ONE WINTER

A grizzly bear waits for spring

Winter has fallen on the alpine forest, covering the great pine and spruce trees with a thick layer of snow. Underground in his den, barely visible for the rocks and fallen branches that secure its entrance, a grizzly bear is settling in for winter.

He has been busy all year, building up his fat reserves and digging and fetching materials from the forest for bedding. Now he retreats into a type of slumber, hibernating for up to seven months without the need for food or water.

Just as we patiently wait for nature to thaw and show promise of life, Grizzly Bear rests until spring arrives again . . .

Winter arrives.

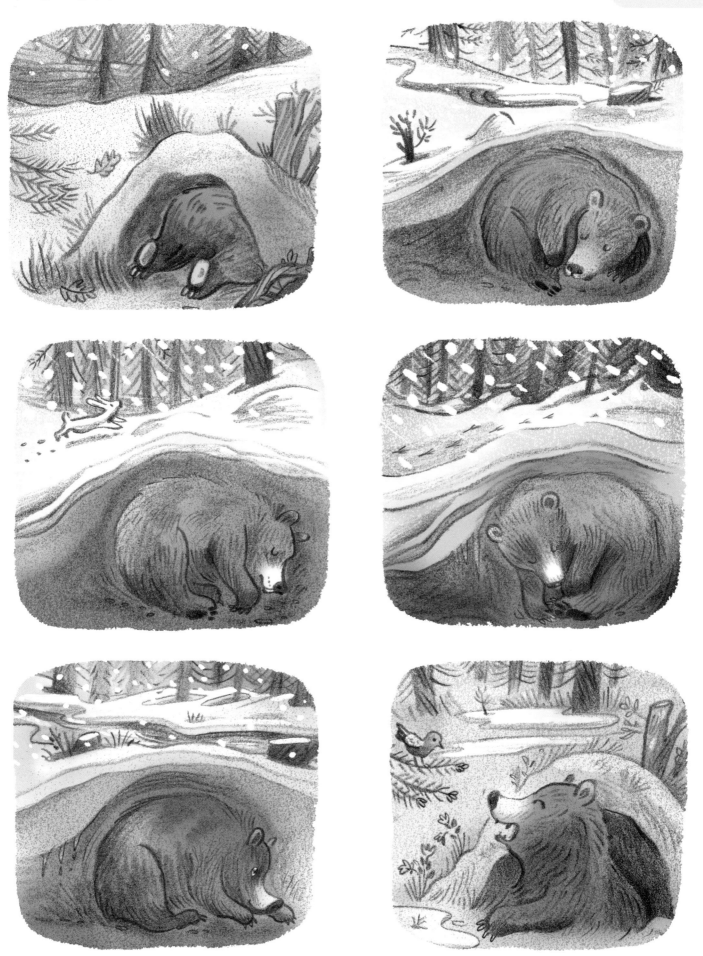

Spring is finally here!

WINTER SLUMBER

The familiar route through the forest is colder today.
Fall has given way to *WINTER* snow.

In a forest just like this one, high up on a mountainside, a grizzly bear knows by the first big snowstorm that it is time to retreat. A small opening in the deepest part of the forest is where this grizzly has made his winter home.

Deep inside the den, the bear's thick coat makes for perfect winter wear. Icicles hang from fences, and the thought of toasting marshmallows by a fire hurries you home. But Grizzly Bear still slumbers, his fat reserves keeping him well fed as he waits . . .

As the months pass by, the snowy pathways melt away. The den remains silent and still ... but in the valley, the birds start to busy themselves.

From spring to autumn, hungry GRIZZLY BEARS spend their time eating, resting, and mating. They use the warmer weather to gather food sources and build up their fat reserves, which will enable them to survive the winter.

Vivid green grass and wildflowers now line the familiar path. Finally, high up in the still-snowy mountains, Grizzly Bear is waking up ...

As Grizzly Bear emerges from his den, he turns to face the SPRING sunshine. He yawns and breathes in the warming air, before venturing out onto the thawing snow, one slow, sleepy step at a time.

IN NINE MONTHS

A baby is born

All living things on Earth are born from reproduction. Some life-forms can reproduce on their own, but humans and most animals need two parents to join together.

For humans, when a cell from the mother and a cell from the father have joined to form a new cell, the journey of life has begun. Over the course of nine months, the new cell—called a zygote—will divide in the mother's womb, becoming an embryo, then a fetus. It will change and develop until the baby is fully grown and ready to emerge into the world.

From a zygote . . .

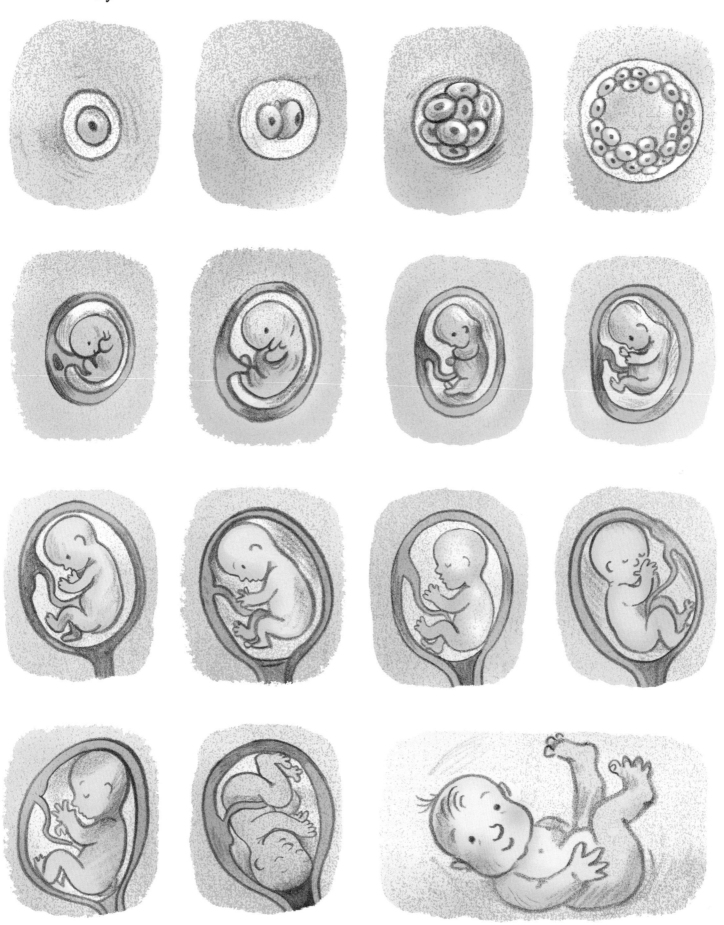

. . . to a baby!

FROM EMBRYO TO BABY

A single female cell, an *EGG*, is fertilized by a single male cell, a *SPERM*. This union creates an embryo which will grow into a fetus and then a baby. So begins the journey of life!

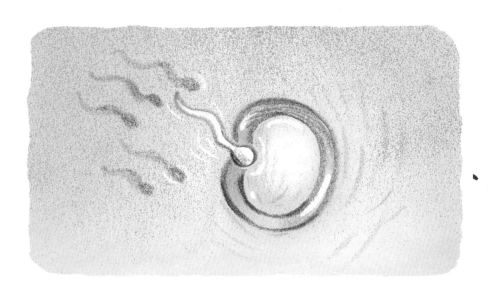

The embryo is protected by a *FLUID SAC*, and the *PLACENTA* starts to form. The placenta is a lifeline—it connects the baby to its mother, providing all the oxygen and nutrients the baby needs to grow.

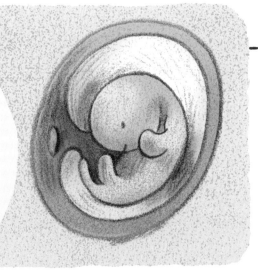

When the egg and sperm meet, a *ZYGOTE* is formed. The zygote stage is short, lasting about four days, and from this moment cells divide and produce over and over again.

The baby is as tiny as a tadpole, but its body starts to *DEVELOP* and form. Soon a tiny heart, lungs, fingers, and toes emerge. Eyes and ears are appearing. After a few more weeks, it's as big as a lime!

By the fourth month of pregnancy, it can move and kick and make its presence felt. Its fingernails and hair are growing. It has a nervous system that is starting to function. Hair protects its head, and a waxy white coating called *VERNIX* protects its soft skin.

It's the sixth month. Baby can hear now! Its mother's voice booms through the walls of her uterus.

Baby is as big as a cauliflower. Its lungs are getting stronger; its limbs are growing longer. Its mother's body is working very hard to prepare the baby for *BIRTH*.

It's been 40 weeks now. Baby's head nestles lower in its mother's body as it gets ready to be *BORN*.

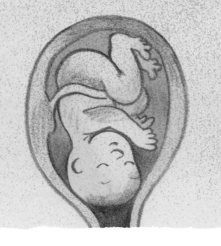

Welcome to the world, baby!

IN ONE YEAR

An apple tree grows fruit

Apple trees are growing and changing all the time—
just like you and me. It takes a whole year for an apple to
transform from bud to fruit, over four busy seasons.

Every year, the apple tree will produce a different
amount of fruit. To thrive, the tree will need plenty
of sun, a little shade, and well-drained, moist soil.
It cleverly knows exactly what to do each season,
and how to work with the weather and to
repeat the cycle again and again.

The year begins . . .

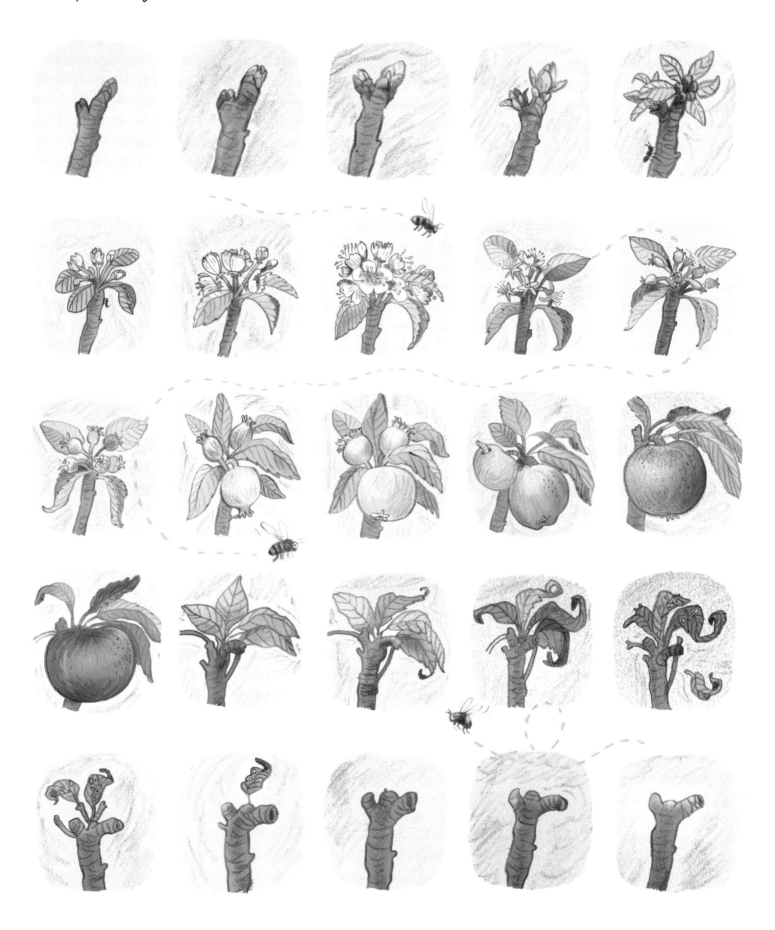

. . . and ends, ready to begin again.

A YEAR around an APPLE TREE

In the depths of WINTER, the apple tree preserves its energy to soak up nutrients from the ground. Tiny buds along the branches are covered in a light fuzz, which protects them from the cold.

As the weather gets warmer, buds start to sprout with leaves and apple blossom flowers, signaling the arrival of EARLY SPRING. This is key pollination season, when bees and other insects enjoy the nectar from the tree's flowers, coating themselves in yellow pollen, before flying to another apple tree to feed from its flowers.

By LATE SPRING the tree's blossom has started to fall and, in its place, fruit buds appear.

When **SUMMER'S SUN** arrives, the tree is heavy with green apples, which grow and ripen during the long, warm days.

As **AUTUMN** sets in, the apple tree's leaves turn gold. Apple Tree has one final job for its fruit, as it helps turn their starch into sugar, so that they become ripe and delicious to eat. Each one will be harvested before the very last leaf has dropped.

Most apple trees grow slowly and don't produce fruit immediately. Most start to produce **FRUIT** in their third or fourth year.

53

IN TWENTY-FIVE YEARS

A coral reef starts to form

Deep below the surface of the tropical waters is a magical underwater kingdom, a unique ecosystem filled with fascinating life-forms and colorful creatures. Welcome to the enchanting world of a hard coral reef.

Although hard coral may look like rock, it is in fact a living colony of hundreds of thousands of coral polyps—small, soft sea animals with tentacles, a mouth, a stomach, and a nerve-net (their nervous system). A single coral polyp will grow and mature over twenty-five years, and go on to live for hundreds and even thousands of years to come if protected and left to its own natural devices.

. . . to a thriving coral colony!

TWENTY-FIVE YEARS *of* CHANGE

A coral reef begins when coral polyps bud and form more polyps, slowly creating what we call a reef, or a coral colony. It takes around twenty-five years, or a quarter of a century, for this transformation to occur.

Once fertilized, these little larvae drift back down and land on the sea bed, sometimes settling on a rock, where they take root. Now they will grow into coral polyps.

In the shallows, tiny coral gametes (reproductive cells) are released into the water by the coral on the ocean floor. They bubble up to the surface and float on the water's edge.

Once the young coral polyps have grown mouths and tentacles, they produce a rocky, chalklike substance called calcium carbonate. This forms a hard, protective skeleton around their soft bodies. The hard coral polyps cluster together in groups, or colonies.

Over decades, the coral polyps grow and bloom. Buds appear! Like the branches of a tree, the coral reaches out in all directions. Layer upon layer of new coral polyps take root, until a whole coral reef is born.

Coral skeletons are white, like bones. Their colors come from microscopic algae living in the coral's cells. The algae contain a pigment called chlorophyll, which transforms the reef into a rich rainbow of pinks, reds, greens, and browns.

This story is about **HARD CORAL**, but **SOFT CORALS** also live in tropical waters. They have a jellylike, fleshy structure, that bends and waves with the motion of the water.

57

IN THIRTY YEARS

A century plant blooms

In a hot, dry desert in Mexico, a blue-green century plant has been growing for decades. But before it reaches the end of its life, it has a surprise . . .

For nearly thirty years, the spiky, spiny leaves of this succulent agave plant have flourished. But now, it uses up the last of its energy to send a single flowering stalk skyward, topped with vivid yellow blossoms. What a show-stopper! After this once-in-a-lifetime bloom, the leaves at the plant's base wither away and die. But it's not the end! A new generation of baby agave pups remain, to begin the cycle all over again.

What starts as a tiny bud . . .

. . . grows into a towering bloom!

59

A THIRTY-YEAR BLOOM

Contrary to its name, the century plant blooms just once every thirty years or so. This giant of the plant world starts its life as a tiny seed . . .

As a seedling, the century plant looks like any other desert plant, with smooth, spiny-edged leaves—and it's small enough to hold in your hands!

The century plant is native to Mexico and southern North America but can thrive in hot places, with plenty of space, sunlight, and the right amount of water.

Over the years, the plant grows taller. Its leaves become larger and much sharper!

Thirty years have passed. Finally, a single stalk shoots up from the middle of the plant's leaves. It's finally ready to bloom! It has taken all of the plant's remaining energy to produce this incredible show.

Towering over all that gather, the stalk is topped with vibrant yellow blossoms. At long last the century plant's colorful bloom takes center stage.

After the blooms die back, so too will this plant, but its babies will begin the cycle all over again.

The leaves of the
CENTURY PLANT
produce fibers, which are used to make rope, nets, and baskets. They also contain a sweet syrup called
AGAVE NECTAR.

IN SIXTY YEARS

A patch of rainforest regrows

A squawk pierces the air. There's a flash of bright orange feathers. A tree shakes, and a long, fuzzy tail disappears into the canopy. Nowhere else on Earth boasts such a diverse display of life as a tropical rainforest.

From the rich soil of the forest floor to high above the trees, this haven for wildlife is resilient, but under constant threat from fire, deforestation, and climate change. But if left alone, a patch of rainforest will regrow within around sixty years. In just over a century it will have recovered entirely, showing us that nature can overcome almost anything . . .

Fire has swept through the rainforest...

...but if left alone, it will regrow and flourish.

SIXTY YEARS *of* GROWTH . . .

A patch of *RAINFOREST* lays bare after a fierce forest fire. In this wild habitat, the soil is made up of decomposing plants and living organisms, as well as carbon and minerals. It is a perfect foundation for new life.

TWENTY-FIVE YEARS have passed, and a carpet of green has taken over the forest floor. New trees have taken root, and insects weave between them.

One tall shoot stands among the greenery: it's a kapok tree! It has a long, spindly trunk and pointed leaves that look like the palm of a hand.

It is now *FORTY YEARS* since the fire. The forest floor is dark and humid and covered in ferns and fungi. Birds fly through the canopy, and a spider monkey swings between the branches of the kapok tree. It is much taller now, and its pink flowers are in bloom. A snake slithers down the tree trunk and disappears into a crevice in the kapok's roots.

Rainforests cover about six percent of *EARTH'S SURFACE*. The world's largest rainforest is the Amazon, in South America. It's estimated nearly *400 BILLION TREES* live here!

It's *SIXTY YEARS* since the fire. The canopy is so thick that the sky is barely visible. Butterflies trail vibrant colors as they flit from leaf to flower. A long line of busy ants crosses your path. A combination of warmth and heavy rainfall have helped this lush ecosystem thrive.

IN SEVENTY YEARS

An African savanna elephant grows old

A shrill trumpet sound pierces the air. A precious baby elephant has been born. Just twenty minutes after its birth, this calf—the largest land animal in the world—will take its first steps, the first of many in a very long life to come.

The herd is thirsty and on the move. An elephant's memory spans decades—nearly seven of them—which serves the herd well during the dry season, as the older elephants remember exactly where to find fresh water and food on the vast savanna grasslands.

From newborn baby...

...to wise, old elephant.

67

AN ELEPHANT'S LIFE CYCLE

BABY ELEPHANT takes her first wobbly steps through the dry grass. *Oops!* She falls down, but with help from her mom's strong trunk, it doesn't take long for her to pull herself back up using her front legs.

At first, she stays close to her mother, copying what she does and wrapping her trunk around Mom's legs for comfort.

TEN YEARS have passed, and the elephant plays in the waterhole, swishing her trunk back and forth in the muddy waters. This is her way of cooling down in the blazing African sun.

By **FIFTEEN YEARS OLD** the elephant is a grown-up and has a baby of her own. She walks with her baby, trunk to tail, just like she did with her mother. It hasn't rained for weeks, so the herd is on the march again. They keep going for many days until they reach water.

Our elephant is now **SEVENTY YEARS OLD**. The wrinkles in her thick skin are even deeper now. She dozes as she stands in the shade of an acacia tree, flapping her enormous ears to stay cool. She will spend many of her summers here, resting after such a long life wandering the savanna.

There are three species of elephant: the **AFRICAN FOREST**, the **AFRICAN SAVANNA**, and the **ASIAN** elephant. African elephants have much bigger ears than their Asian cousins!

IN AROUND EIGHTY YEARS

A human lives a lifetime

The average person lives between seventy and eighty years, but many millions of people have the great fortune to live even longer. So much is possible in a human lifetime—from the moment a baby is born, it's hard to imagine all the things that could happen along the way.

As we grow, our bodies and minds evolve, changing from one year to the next. And while every person's journey is unique, we all hope to remain happy and healthy for as long as we live.

So much is possible in a single lifetime!

THE JOURNEY of a LIFETIME

Lub-dub, lub-dub . . . a heartbeat is heard from deep within this mother's womb, signaling new life. In just a few months a baby will enter the world, with kicking legs and a hungry belly!

Not long after a baby is born, it can crawl, toddle, fall, and get back up again. These early years are full of tears, laughter, and lots of learning.

Time to play!

As we grow, friends become like family— they comfort and inspire us . . .

Arms and legs grow stronger, allowing us to take on exciting new adventures!

The power of biology takes over, and our bodies surprise us with new, incredible changes every day. *HORMONES* drive our development. We are getting ready to go out into the world with our own ideas.

As we move into ADULTHOOD, we become independent and take on new responsibilities. We begin building our home and our world.

Later, we will have time to reflect on who we have become and all we have done. Our family, friends, and experiences help to create a rich life full of ups and downs, highs and lows, and lots of love.

Our eyes are now creased around the edges, but they shine with wisdom.

You will see close to 29,000 sunsets in your LIFETIME if you live to 78 years old.

Our bones change and become creakier. We seem smaller on the outside, but our heart and soul are bigger than ever on the inside.

IN OVER ONE HUNDRED YEARS

*A Galápagos giant tortoise
completes its life cycle*

Nature is forever on the move. From a single minute to a full century, hearts beat, light travels from the sun, the moon rises and sets, birds hunt prey and lay eggs. Coral transforms into magnificent reefs, rainforests regenerate, babies are born, elephants grow old—and so do we! And each of these magical moments happens within the lifetime of one very special creature: the Galápagos giant tortoise.

As this book draws to a close, think about the many fascinating stories you have read and the amazing animals and humans you have encountered along the way. Now it's time to meet the oldest of them all . . .

A tiny tortoise hatchling . . .

. . . can live for a whole century!

A GIANT LIFE

Across a sandy clearing on the Galápagos Islands, tucked away behind a clump of trees, is a nest. Sixteen white EGGS lie safe and warm beneath the soil. And one of them is starting to hatch . . .

As a crack opens across the shell, a tiny face with beady eyes appears. A Galápagos giant tortoise HATCHLING nuzzles its way into the world.

After only ONE MONTH, this baby ventures off alone, leaving the nest and her siblings behind.

TEN YEARS have passed, and the Galápagos tortoise moves slowly through the forest, grazing and resting as she pleases. She stretches her long neck and tugs on a green vine with her strong jaws. *Munch! Munch!*

At TWENTY-FIVE YEARS OLD and four feet long, Galápagos Tortoise is now fully grown and ready for babies of her own.

It's mating season. She moves to higher ground, searching for food—and a mate!

Back down in the lowlands, our tortoise looks for the safest spot to lay her eggs. After days of digging with her strong back legs, she creates a nest.

Once she has laid her eggs, she covers them with wet mud and leaves, to seal them in. The young will be safe in here for a few months until they hatch...

Throughout her long lifetime, our tortoise will return each time she's ready to lay more eggs.

Galápagos Tortoise moves even more slowly now, sleeping for many hours each day. At 100 YEARS OLD she has one of the longest lifespans of all known vertebrates.

Wild Galápagos tortoises may live to be 150 YEARS OLD. Captive tortoises live even longer. One female, named Harriet, lived to be 176!

INDEX

For my love, Erik, who knows
how to wait —RW

For lovely Joy, who had time
for everyone xxx —LL

FURTHER READING

Slow Down: 50 Mindful Moments in Nature
written by Rachel Williams
and illustrated by Freya Hartas

Slow Down and Be Here Now:
More Nature Stories to Make You Stop, Look,
and Be Amazed by the Tiniest Things
written by Laura Brand
and illustrated by Freya Hartas

Life Cycles: Everything from Start to Finish
written by DK and illustrated by Sam Falconer

Waiting
by Kevin Henkes

A Butterfly Is Patient
by Dianna Hutts Aston
and illustrated by Sylvia Long

Here We Are: Notes for Living on Planet Earth
by Oliver Jeffers

Hundred: What You Learn in a Lifetime
written by Heike Faller and illustrated
by Valerio Vidali

The illustrations in this book were created in pencil and colored digitally.
Set in Macho, Ammer Handwriting, Alburgone, BillyShakes5, and The Secret Things.

Library of Congress Control Number 2023952507
ISBN 978-1-4197-7463-8

Text © 2024 Rachel Williams
Illustrations © 2024 Leonie Lord
Book design by Maisy Ruffels
Cover © Magic Cat 2024

First published in the United Kingdom in 2024 by Magic Cat Publishing Ltd. First published in North America
in 2024 by Magic Cat Publishing, an imprint of ABRAMS. All rights reserved. No portion of this book may be
reproduced, stored in a retrieval system, or transmitted in any form or by any means, mechanical, electronic,
photocopying, recording, or otherwise, without written permission from the publisher.

Printed and bound in China
10 9 8 7 6 5 4 3 2 1

Abrams books are available at special discounts when purchased in quantity for premiums and promotions
as well as fundraising or educational use. Special editions can also be created to specification. For details,
contact specialsales@abramsbooks.com or the address below.

ABRAMS The Art of Books
195 Broadway, New York, NY 10007
abramsbooks.com